Nature's Children

OCTOPUSES

Paul Thompson

GROLIER

j 594.56
Thompson

FACTS IN BRIEF

Classification of Octopuses

Class: *Cephalopoda* (cephalopods)

Order: *Octopoda* (octopus); *Vampyromorphida* (vampire squid)

Suborder: *Incirrata* (octopus); *Cirrata* (finned octopus).

Family: There are 9 families of *Incirrata*. Most belong to the huge family *Octopodidae,* including *Octopus vulgaris* (common octopus). There are 5 families of *Cirrata*.

Genus: There are 48 genera of octopuses.

Species: There are more than 200 species of octopuses.

World distribution.   Oceans and seas throughout the world.

Habitat.   From shallow coastal waters to dark ocean depths.

Distinctive physical characteristics.   Soft head and body with eight flexible arms lined with suckers.

Habits.   Solitary creatures active during the night.

Diet.   A variety of sea creatures, including clams, snails, crabs, and other shellfish.

© 2004 The Brown Reference Group plc
Printed and bound in U.S.A.
Edited by John Farndon and Angela Koo

Published by:

**An imprint of Scholastic Library Publishing
Old Sherman Turnpike, Danbury, Connecticut 06816**

Library of Congress Cataloging-in-Publication Data
Thompson, Paul, 1967–
    Octopuses / Paul Thompson.
      p. cm. — (Nature's children)
    Includes index.
    Summary: Describes the physical characteristics, habits, and natural environment of octopuses.
    ISBN 0–7172–5957–9 (set)   ISBN 0–7172–5970–6
    1. Octopuses—Juvenile literature. [1. Octopuses.] I. Title. II. Series.

QL430.3.O2T48 2004
594'.56—dc21

                           2003049170

Contents

What animal has eight arms, hundreds of suckers, and can travel along using jets of water? It sounds like a creature from another planet, but it's not—it's an octopus.

Because octopuses look strange, many people are frightened of them. Seafarers used to tell scary stories about giant octopuses attacking ships. But very few octopuses are dangerous to people. Most are not very big, and some are very small indeed.

An octopus can change color in the blink of an eye and can squeeze its bendy body into very narrow spaces. Some octopuses can make themselves look like other animals. A few deep-sea octopuses glow in the dark. Scientists have even taught octopuses to do tricks. Octopuses are among the most intelligent animals under the sea.

Octopuses usually blend in with their surroundings. But when they are worried, they may go bright red like this to shock enemies.

Family Tree

Scientists put animals into groups to show how they are related. Animals that are similar are put in the same groups. Octopuses belong to a big group called the mollusks. This group includes animals such as slugs, snails, and clams. Mollusks have a muscular foot, and many also have shells. The mollusk group is very big, so it is divided into smaller groups.

Octopuses belong to a smaller group of mollusks called the cephalopods (pronounced SEH-fuh-luh-pods). The cephalopods have a large head and a mouth at the front surrounded by many arms. The animals in the cephalopod group include octopuses, squids, cuttlefishes, and nautiluses. There are far more than 700 species (types) of cephalopods, and about 200 of them are octopuses. The octopuses are also divided into those without fins and those with fins. Only about 30 octopuses have fins, so most are in the first group.

Head-foot

An octopus has a head, but it doesn't have a neck. It has eight arms joined directly to its large, soft head. The arms are really one big muscular foot divided into eight. That gives the family name cephalopod. Cephalopod means "head-foot." The arms are joined to each other near the head with a web of flesh.

An octopus's big eyes are on the front of its head, where you expect them to be. But if you want to find its mouth, you have to look under its arms. There you'll see a small, hard mouth, a bit like a parrot's beak. There you'll find its tiny body, too, just under the mouth. The body is held in a sack of muscle called the mantle. It looks like wrinkled old leather, but it protects the delicate organs inside, including the octopus's heart and its liver.

Many animals have bones to give their body a rigid support. Octopuses rely entirely on their muscles to keep them in shape. But having no bones means they can bend into all kinds of strange shapes.

Opposite page: *Octopuses look almost like flying ballerinas as they swim through the deep.*

Arms and Suckers

Each of the octopus's eight arms is covered with one or two rows of suckers. The arms are used for grabbing hold of food. They are also used for holding onto rocks when the octopus is moving along the seafloor.

The octopus can bend its arms in all kinds of directions and wrap them tightly around objects. If another animal eats one of the arms, the arm will grow back.

The suckers are stretchy and can change shape. The octopus places the sucker on an object, such as a rock or fish, and then tightens muscles in the sucker. That makes the sucker stick to the object. An octopus may have several hundred suckers, and each one is very sensitive. Octopuses use them to feel and taste things. When an octopus finds something tasty to eat, it wraps its arms around it and holds on tightly with its suckers. That stops the prey from getting away.

An octopus's suckers grip so firmly that a victim like this fish has no hope of escape.

Water Jets

If an octopus wants to move really quickly, it can do so using water jets. The octopus fills a space in its mantle with water. Muscles around and along the mantle quickly tighten. That forces the water out quickly.

The water shoots out of the octopus through a narrow tube called a siphon. It makes a jet of water that throws the octopus in the opposite direction at tremendous speed. Using water jets is very useful if the octopus needs to get away from danger quickly.

Usually octopuses don't need to do this to move around. Instead, they crawl across the bottom of the sea using their arms. When they swim using their siphon, they change direction by changing the direction of the siphon.

Night Hunters

Most octopuses hunt at night. They leave the safety of their den and crawl across the ocean floor looking for prey. It is safer to hunt at night when they cannot be seen. Some octopuses hide among rocks or in sand. There they lie and wait for something tasty.

Some species may wave an arm to make it look like a worm. If a crab comes along to eat the "worm," the octopus grabs the crab with its suckers. When an octopus sees a fish, it uses its siphon to jet quickly down. It may then drop right down on top of its victim with arms stretched out like a parachute. Octopuses eat a wide variety of sea animals, including clams, crabs, fish, shrimp, and lobsters. They may sometimes even eat other octopuses.

Eating

Opposite page:
Even a crab with its armored shell cannot survive long in the deadly embrace of an octopus.

If you catch a crab or a shellfish and want to eat it, how do you get inside its hard shell? For octopuses that is no problem. First of all, they poison the crab with their saliva. Then they try to pull it apart using their powerful arms and suckers. If that doesn't work, an octopus may use its tough beak to break up the shell.

If a shell still proves too tough to crack, the octopus is far from defeated. Because then it brings its radula into action. The radula is the octopus's tongue. Unlike a human tongue, the octopus's radula is not soft; it is long and hard, and has a toothed edged. It is more like a carpenter's file! To get into extratough shells, the octopus first softens the shell with saliva. Then it attacks with its radula, rasping away until it bores a hole right through the shell. Once it reaches the soft flesh inside, the octopus injects a poison to keep the shellfish from moving. Finally, it squirts in chemicals that make the victim's flesh so soft it can be sucked right out through the hole.

Octopus Eyes

It's all very well having lots of arms and suckers to catch things with, but you have to be able to find an animal to catch it. Some sea animals can find animals to eat by feeling the water move. Octopuses find food by touch, taste, and smell. They also have very good eyesight. That may not seem unusual, but it is for a mollusk. Most mollusks cannot see very well, if at all. Octopus eyesight is about as good as ours, but octopuses can only see in black and white.

Octopuses can see things about 0.2 inches (0.5 centimeters) long from a distance of 3 feet (1 meter). That is very good for seeing prey. Good eyesight helps the octopus in another way. Lots of sea animals would like to eat octopus, so the octopus uses its eyes to keep a sharp lookout for danger.

Octopuses also use their eyes during mating. When they are courting, octopuses change the color of their skin. Other octopuses see this as changes in shade rather than color. But this change is enough to attract a mate.

Sea Chameleon

Opposite page:
Sometimes an octopus turns bright red to frighten off attackers. It also swells up to make itself as big and scary as it can.

An octopus is very, very good at hiding. You can often swim right past an octopus and not see it at all. That is because an octopus can change its color to blend in with the surrounding rocks and sand. Like chameleons, octopuses can change color quickly. They can change color completely in less than a second.

Usually, octopuses change color to hide from animals that want to eat them. Sometimes, though, an octopus turns bright red to startle off an attacker. Some species of octopuses can also imitate the colors of dangerous sea animals such as lionfish. That also frightens off attackers.

When they want to attract a mate, a few species of female octopuses get a glowing ring around their mouths—like luminous lipstick! In 1999 scientists discovered that one kind of deep-sea octopus has suckers that glow bright blue in the dark, like a row of Christmas lights. They believe these lights lure tiny shellfish called copepods into the octopus's mouth.

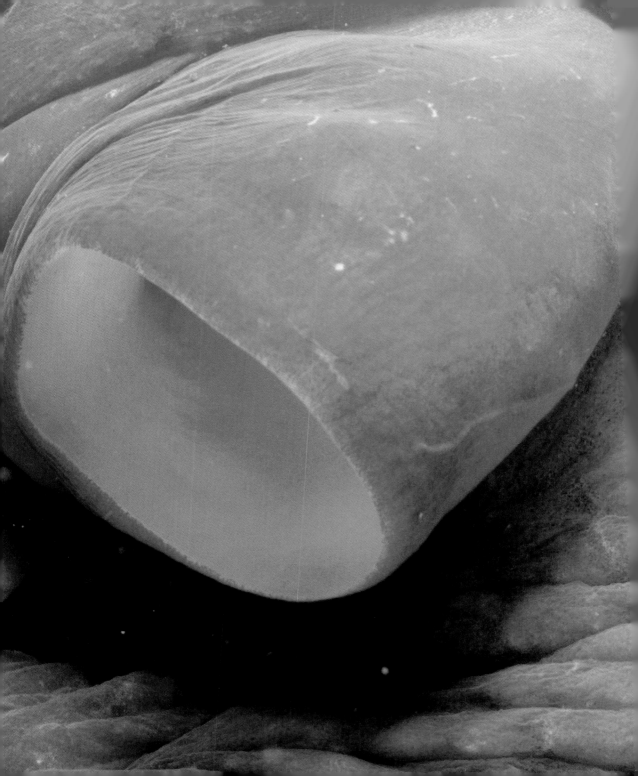

Three Hearts

Most animals make do with one heart, but an octopus has three. The hearts are in the octopus's fleshy mantle. Two of the hearts are called gill-hearts. They are connected to parts of the octopus called gills. Gills are used by octopuses for breathing and are common in many underwater animals. When we breathe, we suck air into our lungs. Oxygen in the air then passes through our lungs and into our blood. When an octopus breathes, it sucks up water into its mantle and over its gills. Oxygen in the water passes through the gills and into the octopus's blood.

The gill-hearts pump the blood through the gills so it can pick up the oxygen. The third heart then pumps the blood and oxygen around the body and arms to where it is needed. Do you think it's strange for an animal to have three hearts? You might be even more surprised to learn that an octopus's blood is not red like our blood; it is blue.

Opposite page:
This is the tube on the side of an octopus's head called the siphon. The siphon squirts out the water the octopus takes in to get oxygen.

Big Brain

Octopuses have very large brains compared with other mollusks. Their big brains make them very intelligent. Octopuses need big brains because they have so many difficult things to do.

The brain must help control the movement of the eight arms. That is difficult because the arms can move around in many directions. The eight arms also have hundreds of suckers. Each one can feel and taste. Doing so takes up a lot of brain power—so much that the octopus has to have brains in its arms as well as its head. The brains in its arms are not true brains but special fibers called nerves. But they help control the arms.

Octopuses are very good at solving problems. In captivity some octopuses have learned how to take the lid off a jar to get to the food inside. They can even find their way around a maze. Octopuses also have good memories. They learn how to do something and then remember how to do it again.

*Inside this octopus's big head is a very big brain,
for a mollusk. For its body weight an octopus has
a bigger brain than quite a few small mammals. It
needs this brain power to help control all those arms.*

Home Alone

Some animals live in groups, but octopuses live alone on the bottom of seas and oceans. Some live in shallow waters. Others live deep down where sunlight cannot reach.

Some octopuses occupy dens between the gaps in rocks and coral. Others use underwater caves for their den. Dens are safe places for octopuses to live. Some octopuses will even block up the entrance to the den with rocks. That helps keep out intruders. When there are no caves or gaps in rocks, octopuses will happily make their home in an old car tire or even a glass bottle.

You can often tell where an octopus lives. Outside the den you can see all the empty shells of the crabs, lobsters, and other shellfish it has eaten. Octopuses don't stay in the same place for long. They may stay in a den for several weeks. Then they move out and find somewhere different to live.

Opposite page: *When they are not out on the prowl, octopuses like to hide away in crevices in the seabed.*

Colorful Courting

Opposite page: *When a male octopus finds a female willing to mate, he extends a long arm toward her.*

Octopuses mate when they are old enough. That is when they are between three months and three years old, depending on the species. Because octopuses live alone, they must search for a mate. Some scientists think they may do that using chemicals. When the female is ready to mate, she releases chemicals. They are carried on ocean currents. Males can follow the smell of the chemicals back to the female.

When the male finds a female, he may encourage her to mate by showing changing color patterns. Showing bright colors can be dangerous, so the Caribbean reef squid may show colors only on the side nearest the female. Eventually the female is ready, and the pair mate. Sometimes, though, she may eat the male afterward!

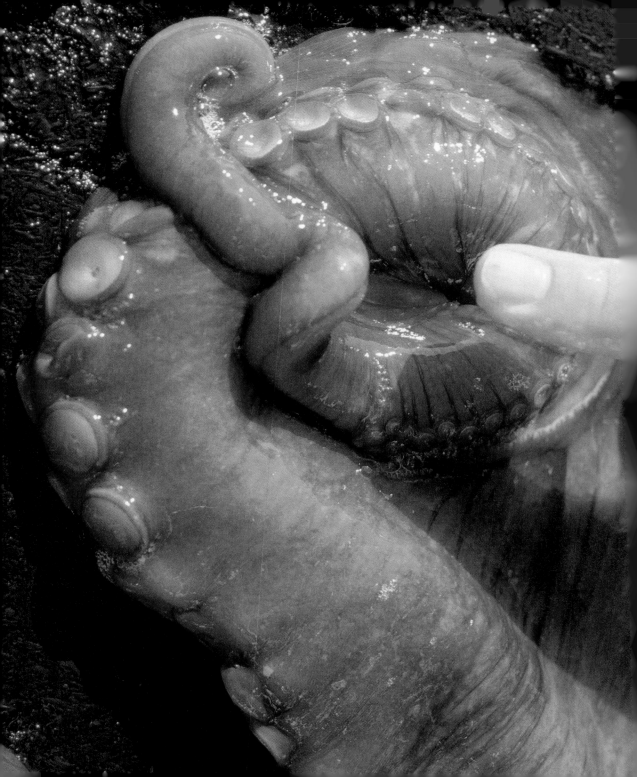

Special Arm

One of the male octopus's eight arms is different than the rest. This special arm is the third one on the octopus's right and is called the hectocotylus (pronounced HEK-toh-KOT-i-luss). The tip of this arm has no suckers. Instead, it is spoon shaped.

When the male and female are mating, the arm fills with sperm. Sperm are male sex cells. The sperm is made inside the body of the octopus. During mating the male puts the hectocotylus inside the female's mantle. Sometimes while all this is going on the female goes on looking around her for food.

Inside the female's mantle sperm fuse with the female's sex cells, or eggs. This is called fertilization. The fertilized eggs are then ready to grow into baby octopuses. Typically, the female octopus holds onto the sperm for up to 100 days before adding it to the eggs to fertilize them. In the meanwhile, she might mate with several other males.

Opposite page: *When mating, a male octopus uses a special arm called the hectocotylus. The tip of this arm— indicated by the pointing finger— fills with sperm and is inserted into the female.*

Egg Care

Opposite page:
A female octopus often lays her eggs on the ceiling of a safe den. She closes up the entrance and looks after them until they are ready to hatch.

A few months after the male and female octopuses have mated, the female lays her eggs. A few octopuses carry their eggs around with them. Most, like the giant octopus, lay their eggs in a den. When the female giant octopus finds a den, she crawls inside and closes up the entrance with stones. She then lays her eggs on the ceiling of the den.

While the eggs are growing, the octopus mom does not eat. She stays inside the den to protect the eggs. She must do so because other animals, such as crabs and starfish, like to eat the eggs. The eggs must also be kept clean. The octopus mom gently uses her suckers to clean the eggs. She also blows a stream of water over the eggs using her siphon. That makes sure the developing octopuses inside the eggs get plenty of oxygen to breathe.

By the time the eggs are ready to hatch, the octopus mom is very weak. She dies as the baby octopuses finally break free of their eggs and swim away to begin their lives.

Young Octopuses

Some species of octopuses lay large eggs. Others, including giant octopuses, lay small eggs. These small octopus babies are no bigger than a grain of rice. They are also so light that they float up to the sea surface. For a month or so they live there and feed on tiny sea creatures called zooplankton (said ZOO-plank-tuhn). Eventually, they grow big and heavy enough to sink to the bottom of the ocean and live as adults.

Larger babies look like tiny versions of their parents right from the start. After hatching, they live on the bottom of the ocean floor. They hide among rocks and crevices, and hunt just like their parents.

Very few octopus hatchlings survive until they become adults. It takes some kinds up to three years to grow to adult size. During that time most are eaten by predators. Only about one or two in 200,000 young octopuses get to grow up and have babies of their own.

Opposite page:
Here are baby spotted octopuses in their eggs ready to hatch. The baby on the left is already emerging.

Deep Down

Opposite page:
*A deep-sea finned,
or cirrate, octopus.*

Deep below the surface of the ocean lives a group of unusual octopuses called the finned octopuses. They look different than their shallow-water cousins. As their name suggests, finned octopuses have fins. There are two fins, one on each side of the octopus's mantle. The webs of finned octopuses also extend farther down the arms than on other octopuses. When a finned octopus has its arms extended, it looks a little like an umbrella.

Finned octopuses move differently than other octopuses. Most octopuses crawl along the ocean floor or shoot along on a jet of water. Finned octopuses move more like jellyfish. They spread out their webbing and then pull it in, forcing water out behind them. This pushes them forward. These creatures may often live as far down as 3,500 feet (1 kilometer) below the surface.

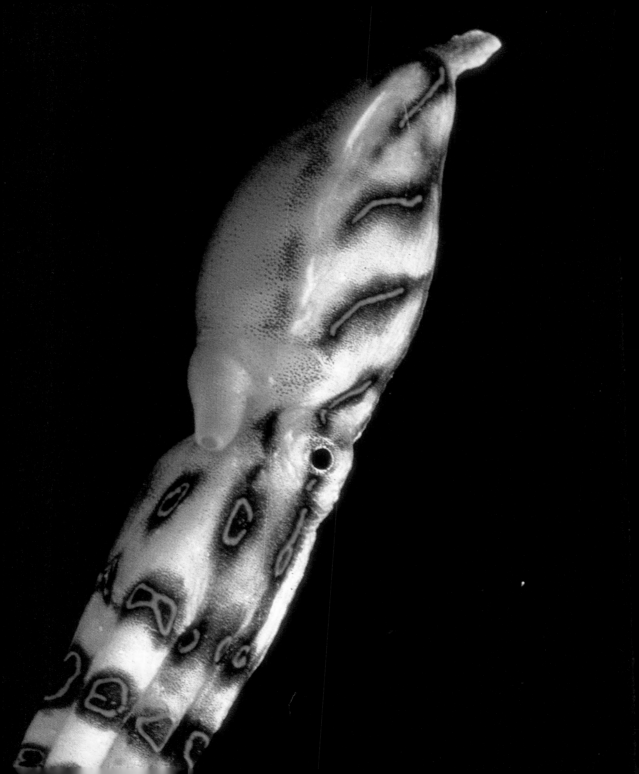

Blue and Deadly

If you see a small octopus with blue rings on its body, don't go near it! It is the blue-ringed octopus of Australia and Southeast Asia. It is the most dangerous octopus and is one of the deadliest animals in the sea.

Most people think that big octopuses are dangerous, but the blue-ringed octopus is very small. If you stretched this octopus out, it would only be 4 inches (10 centimeters) wide. Its bite contains enough poison to kill 20 adults, and there is no known cure. A person can die only 15 minutes after being bitten. This octopus's beak is so sharp it can bite through a diver's rubber wet suit. The deadly venom is not only used in defense. It is also used to kill prey.

Luckily the blue-ringed octopus can be easy to recognize. As its name suggests, its skin is sometimes covered with blue rings. The octopus makes these blue rings shine out when it feels threatened. The rings announce to enemies that it is dangerous.

Opposite page: *This is one of the deadliest of all sea creatures, the blue-ringed octopus of Australia and Southeast Asia. One bite contains enough poison to kill 20 people in just 15 minutes.*

Escape

Opposite page:
This octopus is feeling very threatened by the diver who has grabbed it. So it is sending out a great cloud of black ink. The octopus hopes the ink will hide it while it makes a quick getaway.

Life under the sea can be difficult for an octopus. There is always some bigger, hungry animal that would like to eat it. Octopuses have a number of ways of dealing with these attackers. Sometimes octopuses change color to blend into the rocks and sand. At other times they shoot off using a jet of water. Another good way to escape is to hide behind a cloud of ink, and that is exactly what the octopus does. If a dangerous animal comes close, the octopus squirts a cloud of black ink. It then shoots off, leaving the attacker behind.

Some octopuses change shape as well as color. When they do this, they can make themselves look like another animal. They even move like the animal they are copying. Some scientists think these octopuses change shape to confuse their enemies. Others think the octopuses do it to make themselves look harmless. Then the octopuses can get close to other animals and eat them.

Giant Octopus

Seafarers have often told tales of being attacked by huge octopuses with long arms. These stories are probably not true, but big octopuses can look pretty scary. The biggest octopus in the world is the giant octopus. Giant octopuses live in the Pacific Ocean from shallow waters to as far down as 1,650 feet (500 meters).

If you stretch a giant octopus out and measure from the tip of one arm to the tip of another arm, it measures about 16 feet (5 meters). The biggest giant octopus ever found had a span of 31 feet (9.6 meters) and weighed about 600 pounds (270 kilograms)— with arms as long as a Cadillac and a brain as big as a grizzly bear's brain.

Most giant octopuses weigh around 15 to 20 pounds (7 to 9 kilograms). They live for up to four years. That is longer than most octopuses, but giant octopuses still have to grow very quickly to reach such a big size.

Opposite page: *Giant octopuses like this are enormous, with 280 suckers on each of their huge arms, and a head as big as a human diver.*

Octopus Relatives

Opposite page:
Cuttlefish get their name from their internal shell, or cuttlebone. It acts like a buoyancy tank to help them move up and down through the water.

Squid and cuttlefish are close relatives of octopuses. They are all cephalopods. Squid and cuttlefish have eight arms like octopuses. They also have two spoon-shaped arms called tentacles. They shoot them out to catch prey.

Octopuses mostly move by crawling along the ocean floor. Squid and cuttlefish usually travel by flapping their fins and squirting jets of water. Squid can swim very fast. Some species can travel as fast as 24 miles per hour (40 kilometers per hour). Some squid also grow much bigger than octopuses. The giant squid can grow to be 53 feet (16 meters) long.

Cuttlefish have a shell inside their body called a cuttlebone. It is full of tiny pockets of gas. The cuttlefish can vary the amount of gas in the cuttlebone to help it move up or down through the water. The cuttlefish sucks gas from the pockets to help it float up and pumps it back in to sink again. This is a very slow process. Like octopuses, cuttlefish use a cloud of ink to escape from attackers.

Vampire Squid

The vampire squid is a close relative of the octopus. It is a strange kind of cephalopod with spikes on its arms.

When the vampire squid was first discovered, scientists counted eight arms and so decided it was an octopus. Scientists later discovered it had two more arms. That made it more like a squid, which has eight arms and two tentacles. But the vampire squid's extra arms are not quite like a squid's tentacles. So scientists decided that it is not really a squid or an octopus. It is something in between.

Vampire squid live thousands of feet below the surface of tropical seas. Sunlight cannot reach down into these ocean depths. In these pitch-black waters vampire squid make their own light. Parts of their skin glow in the dark. In a place without light glow-in-the-dark skin is probably good for attracting food. Biologists think that small animals are drawn to the light like moths to a flame. Making light is probably good for finding a mate, too.

Words to Know

Cephalopod Group of related mollusks with arms or tentacles, including octopuses, squid, and cuttlefish.

Gill The part of an octopus used for breathing.

Gill-hearts Two of the octopus's three hearts. They pump blood through the gills.

Hectocotylus An arm on a male octopus, used in mating.

Mantle The sack covering the fleshy body of an octopus.

Mollusks A group of animals that includes octopuses and other animals such as slugs and snails, oysters, and clams.

Radula A long, hard strip in an octopus's mouth covered in tiny teeth. It can be used like a file.

Siphon Tube on an octopus that it uses to shoot out water.

Species A particular type of animal.

Sperm Male sex cells. Sperm fuse with female's eggs to produce young.

Sucker Pad that clings by suction.

Tentacle A long, bendy organ used for capturing prey.

Venom Poison injected by animals to kill prey or for defense.

Webbing Skin between an octopus's arms, used to push against the water to help the animal move.

Zooplankton Very tiny sea creatures that float in the water.

INDEX